૮/૩/૬૧

D1190784

THE OPEN WORLD

THE
OPEN WORLD

THREE LECTURES ON THE METAPHYSICAL IMPLICATIONS OF SCIENCE

BY

DR. HERMANN WEYL

OX BOW PRESS
Woodbridge, Connecticut

1989 reprint published by:
OX BOW PRESS
P.O. Box 4045
Woodbridge, Connecticut 06525

The paper used in this publication meets the minimum re-
quirements of American National Standard for Information
Sciences – Permanence of Paper for Printed Library Materials,
ANSI Z39.48-1984.
∞

Library of Congress Cataloging-in-Publication Data

Weyl, Hermann, 1885–1955.
    The open world : three lectures on the metaphysical
implications of science / by Hermann Weyl.
        p.   cm.
    Reprint. Originally published: New Haven : Yale University
Press, 1932.
    1. Science—Philosophy.   2. Religion and science—
1926–1945.   3. Causation.   4. Infinite.   I. Title.
Q175.W54   1989
501—dc19   89–3049
                                                         CIP

ISBN 0–918024–71–4
ISBN 0–918024–70–6 (pbk.)

Printed in the United States of America

PREFACE

ONE common thought holds together the following three lectures: Modern science, insofar as I am familiar with it through my own scientific work, mathematics and physics make the world appear more and more as an open one, as a world not closed but pointing beyond itself. Or, as Franz Werfel expresses it in pregnant wording in one of his poems,

"Diese Welt ist nicht die Welt allein."

Science finds itself compelled, at once by the epistemological, the physical and the constructive-mathematical aspect of its own methods and results, to recognize this situation. It remains to be added that science can do no more than show us this open horizon; we must not by including the transcendental sphere attempt to establish anew a closed (though more comprehensive) world.

I am grateful to Yale University for affording me an opportunity in these Terry Lectures of expressing this conviction by a description of the methodology of mathematics and physics. The lectures were originally written out in German. I do not want to omit acknowledging my indebtedness to my friend, Dr. Lulu Hofmann of Columbia University, New York, for the devoted assistance which she has rendered me in the translation of my manuscripts into English on this as well as on similar previous occasions.

H. W.

Yale University
April 15, 1931

CONTENTS

Preface v
I. God and the Universe 1
II. Causality 31
III. Infinity 57

I

GOD AND THE UNIVERSE

A MATHEMATICIAN steps before you, speaks about metaphysics, and does not hesitate to use the name of God. That is an unusual practice nowadays. The mathematician, according to the ideas of the modern public, is occupied with very dry and special problems, he carries out increasingly complicated calculations and more and more intricate geometrical constructions, but he has nothing to do with those decisions in spiritual matters which are really essential for man. In other times this was different. Pythagoras, whose figure almost merges into the darkness of mythology, by his fundamental doctrine that the essence of things dwells in numbers, became at the same time the head of a mathematical school and the founder of a religion. Plato's profoundest metaphysical doctrine, his doctrine of ideas, was clad in mathematical garb when he expounded it in rigorous form; it was a doctrine of ideal numbers, through which the mind was to apprehend the structural composition of the world. The spatial figures and relations investigated by geometry—half notional category, half sense perception—were to him the mediators between the phenomenon and the idea. He refused admission to the academy to those who were not trained in mathematics. To Plato, the mathematical lawfulness and harmony of nature ap-

peared as a divine mind-soul. The following words
are from the twelfth book of the *Laws:*

There are two things which lead men to believe in the
Gods: one is our knowledge about the soul, as being the most
ancient and divine of all things; and the other is our knowledge concerning the regularity of the motion of the stars
and all the other bodies.

The present opinion is just the opposite of what once
prevailed among men, that the sun and the stars are without
soul. Even in those days men wondered about them, and that
which is now ascertained was then conjectured by some who
had a more exact knowledge of them—that if they had been
things without soul, and had no mind (νοῦς), they could never
have moved with numerical exactness so wonderful; and even
at that time some ventured to hazard the conjecture that mind
was the orderer of the universe. But these same persons
again mistaking the nature of the soul, which they conceived
to be younger and not older than the body, once more over-
turned the world, or rather, I should say, themselves; for
the bodies which they saw moving in heaven all appeared to
be full of stones and earth and many other lifeless substances, and to these they assigned the causes of all things.
Such studies gave rise to much atheism and perplexity, and
the poets took occasion to be abusive. . . . But now, as I
said, the case is reversed.

No man can be a true worshiper of the Gods who does not
know these two principles—that the soul is the oldest of all
things which are born, and is immortal and rules over all
bodies; moreover, as I have now said several times, he who
has not contemplated the mind of nature which is said to
exist in the stars, and gone through the previous training,
and seen the connection of music with these things, and har-

monized them all with laws and institutions, is not able to give a reason for such things as have a reason.

The cosmology of Aristotle, with its distinction between the terrestrial sublunar domain and the heavenly sphere set into revolution by the "unmoved primal mover," in combination with the Ptolemaic world system which places the earth in the center of the universe, forms the fixed frame into which the medieval church built its dogma of God, Savior, angels, man, and Satan. Dante's *Divina Commedia* is not only a poem of great visionary power, but it contains a bold theological and geometrical construction of the cosmos, by means of which Christian philosophy adapts Aristotle's cosmology to its own use. While the Aristotelian universe is inclosed by a sphere, the crystal sphere, beyond which there is no further space, Dante lets the radii emanating from the center of the earth, the seat of Satan, converge toward an opposite pole, the source of divine force, much as on the sphere the circles of longitude radiating from the south pole reunite at the north pole. The force of the personal God must radiate from a center, it cannot embrace the world sphere reposing in spatial quiescence like the "unmoved primal mover" of Aristotle. To sense perception, of course, Aristotle's description remains valid. The innermost circles, which surround the divine source of light most closely, by being most heavily charged with divine force become spatially most comprehensive and encompass the more removed circles. In modern mathematical language we would say that Dante propounds a doctrine which in our days has been reestablished by Einstein for entirely different reasons, the doctrine, namely, that three-dimensional space is closed, after the manner of a two-dimensional spherical surface; but from the pole of divine force there radiates a metric field of such a nature that spatial measurement leads to the conditions described by Aristotle.

The Aristotelian world concept was shaken by Copernicus, who recognized the relativity of motion. How could this knowledge, epistemological and mathematical in character and of such complexity that the precise formulation of it even now surpasses the average man's capacity for abstraction—in spite of its being taught, in a somewhat coarse and dogmatic form, of course, in our schools—how could this insight inaugurate a new era in natural philosophy? Only through its coalescence with a certain religious attitude of man toward the universe; for it deprived the earth, the dwelling place of mankind, of its absolute prerogative. The act of redemption by the Son of God, crucifixion and resurrection are no longer the unique cardinal point in the history of the world, but a hasty performance in a little corner of the universe repeating itself from star to star: this blasphemy displays perhaps in the most pregnant manner the precarious aspect which a theory removing the earth from the center of the world bears for religion. In this respect Giordano Bruno drew the conclusions with vehement enthusiasm. Aristotle, Ptolemy, and the ecclesiastical dogma were to him the "three-headed scholastic beast" with which he struggled throughout his life of unrest. To him there lay a mighty liberation in the transition from Aristotle's world, inclosed in the crystal sphere and ordered hierarchically according to strictly distinguished forms of being, to the indifferent expanse of infinite Euclidian space which is everywhere of the same constitution and everywhere filled with stars—the concept which is the foundation of the new natural philosophy. In his *Schriften zur Weltanschauung und Analyse des Menschen seit Renaissance und Reformation,* Dilthey says: "The foundation of the more recent European pantheism is the recognition of the homogeneity and the continuous connection of all parts of the universe." Nicolaus Cusanus and Giordano Bruno are the first heralds of the new conception. Like Pythagoras before him, Bruno considers himself the proclaimer of a "Holy Religion" on the ground of a new mathematical cognition. To him the change from the anthropocentric view supported by sense appearance to the cosmo-centric one acquired by astronomy is only one part of the great revolution effected in the human mind by the new Copernican epoch. There corresponds to it an equally deep and thorough revolution in the religious and moral domain. Sensual consciousness has its center in the preservation of the physical existence which is confined between birth and death. With the emancipation from sense appearance as a result of astronomical discoveries and their philosophical utilization, there is connected the elevation of man to the love of God and of his cosmic manifestations. Not until now do we perceive the true perfection of the universe which springs from the relation of its parts to the whole, and thereby relinquish the undue demands made of this divine order, demands which have their source in the desires of the individual to perpetuate his own existence.

The ideas of Bruno, which propagate themselves in their influence on Spinoza and Shaftesbury, lead to a justified, thoroughgoing, valuable, and promising transformation in the religious attitude of occidental Christianity. Religious belief will always center about two issues, the one cosmic in character, emphasizing human dependence on and relationship to the universe; the other personal, involving moral dignity, autonomy and individual responsibility. In both of these respects, however, a change and advance takes place which is demanded by the progress of culture. This seems to have been the conviction also of the founder of these lectures. But the more modern science, especially physics and mathematics, strives to recognize nature as it is in itself or as it comes from God, the more it has to depart from the human, all too human ideas with which we respond to our practical surroundings in the natural attitude of our existence of strife and action. And the more strange and incomprehensible it must necessarily become to those who cannot devote their entire time and energy to the development and readjustment of their theoretical thinking; herein lies the actual and inevi-

table tragedy of our culture. For the philosophical
and metaphysical import of science has not declined
but rather grown through its estrangement from the
naïve world of human conceptions.

So far I have been speaking of astronomical research and cosmological speculation, with reference
to the manner in which our conception of God and
divine action in nature is formed and transformed
together with such speculation. I shall return to this
point later a little more systematically. But quite
aside from the fact that mathematics is the necessary
instrument of natural science, purely mathematical
inquiry in itself, according to the conviction of many
great thinkers, by its special character, its certainty
and stringency, lifts the human mind into closer
proximity with the divine than is attainable through
any other medium. *Mathematics is the science of the
infinite*, its goal the symbolic comprehension of the
infinite with human, that is finite, means. It is the
great achievement of the Greeks to have made the
contrast between the finite and the infinite fruitful
for the cognition of reality. The intuitive feeling for,
the quiet unquestioning acceptance of the infinite, is
peculiar to the orient; but it remains merely an abstract consciousness, which is indifferent to the concrete manifold of reality and leaves it unformed,
unpenetrated. Coming from the orient, the religious
intuition of the infinite, the ἄπειρον, takes hold of the
Greek soul in the dionysic-orphic epoch which precedes the Persian wars. Also in this respect the Persian wars mark the separation of the occident from

the orient. This tension between the finite and the infinite and its conciliation now become the driving motive of Greek investigation; but every synthesis, when it has hardly been accomplished, causes the old contrast to break through anew and in a deepened sense. In this way it determines the history of theoretical cognition to our day.

The connection between the mathematics of the infinite and the perception of God was pursued most fervently by Nicolaus of Cusa, the thinker who as early as the middle of the fifteenth century, sometimes impetuously, sometimes full of prophetic vision, intonated the new melody of thought which with Leonardo, Bruno, Kepler, and Descartes gradually swells into a triumphant symphony. He recognizes that the scholastic form of thinking, Aristotelian logic, which is based on the theorem of the excluded third, cannot, as essentially a logic of the finite, attain the end for which scholasticism employed it: to think the absolute, the infinite. It must always and of necessity break down where the perception of the infinite is in question. Thereby every kind of "rational" theology is rejected, and "mystic" theology takes its place. But Cusanus is beyond the traditional notion of logic as well as the traditional notion of mysticism; for with the same determination with which he denies the cognition of the infinite through the logic of the finite, he denies the possibility of its apprehension through mere feeling. The true love of God is *amor Dei intellectualis*. And to describe the nature and the aim of the intellectual act through which the divine reveals itself to us, Cusanus does not refer to the mystic form of passive contemplation, but rather to mathematics and its symbolic method. *"Nihil veri habemus in nostra scientia nisi nostram mathematicam."* On the one side stands God as the infinite in perfection, on the other side man in his finiteness; but the Faustian urge driving him toward the infinite, his unwillingness to abide with anything once given and attained, is no fault and no *"hybris"* but evidence of his divine destination. This urge finds its simplest expression in the sequence of numbers, which can be driven beyond any place by repeated addition of the one. We witness here a strange occurrence, unique in the history of philosophy: the exactness of mathematics is sought not for its own sake, nor as a basis for an explanation of nature, but to serve as a foundation for a more profound conception of God. Cusanus is one of the epoch-making minds both in theology and mathematics. All wise men, all the most divine and holy teachers, so his work *De docta ignorantia* sets forth, agree that every visible thing is an image of the invisible, which to us is imperceptible except in a mirror and in enigmas. But even if the spiritual in itself remains inaccessible to us, and even if it can never be perceived by us except in images, or symbols, yet we must at least postulate that the symbols themselves contain nothing doubtful or hazy: the symbols must be endowed with the determinateness and the systematic coherence that is possible only on the basis of mathematics. From here the way leads to Leonardo, Kepler, and Galileo who, after two thousand years of mere description of nature, initiate an actual analysis, a theoretical construction of nature with symbolical mathematical means. With regard to the essence of mathematical knowledge, considered as a symbolical *mathesis universalis*, Cusanus had visions, and expressed ideas, which do not recur in more determinate form until the days of Leibniz; visions, indeed, of which we seem to be acquiring full understanding only at present in the latest attempts to master the antinomies of the infinite by purely symbolical mathematics. This subject will be dealt with in the third lecture.

For speculative metaphysicists, according to Galileo's *Saggiatore*, philosophy is like a book, a product of pure imagination, such as the *Iliad* or *Orlando Furioso*, in which it is of little importance whether what is said is true.

But that is not so; for philosophy is written in the great book of nature which is continually open before our eyes, but which no one can read unless he has mastered the code in which it is composed, that is, the mathematical figures and the necessary relations between them.

The ideality of mathematics lifts the human mind to its most sublime height and perfection: the barriers erected between nature and the mind by medieval thought break down before it, in a certain sense even the barriers between the human and the divine intellect. I once more quote Galileo:

It is true that the divine intellect cognizes the mathematical truths in infinitely greater plenitude than does our own (for

it knows them all), but of the few that the human intellect
may grasp, I believe that their cognition equals that of the
divine intellect as regards objective certainty, since man
attains the insight into their necessity, beyond which there
can be no higher degree of certainty.

And Kepler: "The science of space is unique and
eternal and is reflected out of the spirit of God. The
fact that man may partake of it is one of the reasons
why man is called the image of God."

After this historical introduction I turn to the
question which is to be the primary subject of this
lecture: How does the divine manifest itself in nature? As far as I see, this question has been answered
chiefly in two ways in the history of human thought.
Both answers are forceful, but they are essentially
different. The first is more primitive and more objective: the ether is the omnipresence of God in things.
The second is more advanced and more formal: the
mathematical lawfulness of nature is the revelation
of divine reason.

The significance of the ether concept can only be
understood in connection with the fundamental ideas
of the theory of relativity. Space, the manifold of
space points, is a three-dimensional continuum. This
manifold is, to begin with, amorphous, without structure; in this condition nothing about it would be
changed if I subjected it to some continuous defor-
mation such as one might apply to a mass of clay.
Only statements concerning the distinctness or coin-
cidence of points and the continuous connection of
point configurations can be made at this stage. But

beyond that, space is endowed with structure; this becomes apparent in the fact, among others, that we are able to distinguish the straight lines from the curved ones. A point and a direction assigned to this point uniquely determine a line which passes through it and is of the type we characterize by the adjective straight or geodesic. At earlier times it was believed that among the straight lines the class of verticals was in itself distinguished, that space was designed about the direction from above to below as the original one. We know today that this can be the case only in the gravitational field, where the direction of gravity is distinguished as the one which freely falling bodies follow, but that this direction is determined physically and varies with the physical conditions. The direction from above to below is different in Calcutta from what it is in New Haven, and the angle which these directions form with each other would change if the distribution of mass on the earth were changed, for example, by the folding up of a high range of mountains in the neighborhood of Calcutta. This example seems appropriate to make clear the difference between a rigid geometric structure that cannot be influenced by material forces, like the so-called projective structure which makes possible the distinction between straight and curved, and a structure depending on material influences and changeable with them, as exists, for example, in the directional field of gravitation.

In reference to natural phenomena one cannot consider space separately, but one has to connect it with

time. By saying "here-now" we fix a space-time
point or world point by direct specification. We may
mark it by the momentary flash of a spark of light.
The possible world points or places of localization in
space and time form a four-dimensional continuum.

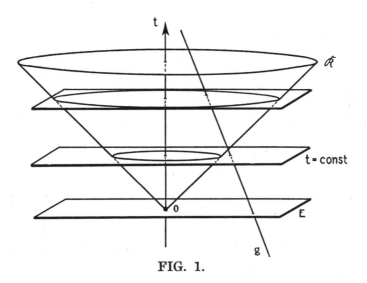

FIG. 1.

A small body describes a world line, the one-dimensional continuum of the world points which it gradually passes through in the course of its history. It
has a meaning directly evident to our intuition only
to say of two events that they occur at the same
space-time position or in immediate space-time proximity. If one believes in a decomposition of the world
into an absolute space and an absolute time, so that
it has a meaning to say of two distinct events, closely

limited in space-time, that they occur at the same place but at different times, or at the same time but at different places, then one is already assigning a definite structure to the four-dimensional extensive medium of the external world. All simultaneous world points form a three-dimensional stratum, all equi-positional world points a one-dimensional fiber. The structure of the world, according to this point of view, can thus be described by stating that it is composed of a stratification traversed by fibers. As long as one cannot refer to a structure of this kind, it is permissible to speak of rest or motion of a body K only with reference to a medium which continuously fills space, or to a body of reference in which K is embedded or on which K lies. In everyday life, the "firm well-founded earth," for good reasons, provides such a body of reference. But who tells us that the earth stands still, or rather, what do we mean by it? The belief that simultaneity exists in the world is originally based on the fact that every person places the events which he perceives in the moment of their perception. But this naïve belief lost its ground long ago through the discovery of the finite velocity of the propagation of light.

The theory of relativity clearly recognized that the structure of the world is not a stratification and fibrillation according to simultaneity and identity of position. It points out: (1) Not rest but uniform translation is an intrinsically distinguished class of motion, uniform translation being the state of motion of a body left to itself and not deviated through the

action of any external forces. The world line of such
a body is uniquely determined by the starting point
and the initial direction of its motion in the world;
the "projective" structure which thus manifests itself
is called by the physicist the inertial guiding field.
The so-called law of inertia, according to which a
body that is left to itself moves through space along a
straight line with constant velocity (into the discussion of which, however, I cannot enter here), conceives the inertial structure as a rigid geometric
entity. (2) The strata of simultaneity are replaced
by a causal structure: from every world point O
there extends into the world a three-dimensional
cone-shaped surface which in the manner evident
from the figure determines a region of the past and
one of the future from O. If I am now at O, the events

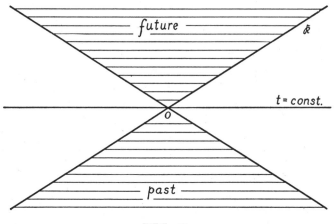

FIG. 2.

on which my actions at O can still be of influence,
i.e., those world points which can be reached by an
action at O, belong to the future, while those events
which exercise an effect upon the events at O are local-
ized in the past. Past events, then, are those of which
I, at O, can somehow receive intelligence through direct perception and tradition or recollection based
upon such perception; for every perception and
every mode of information is a physical transference
of action. But between past and future there extends
an intermediate region with which I am causally connected neither actively nor passively at this moment.
In the old theory past and future touch without in-
tervening space in the stratum of the present, the
ensemble of world points simultaneous with O. The
abstract time relations must be replaced everywhere
by concrete causal connections. The actual motion of
a body results from a conflict between the inertial
guidance and the deviating forces. The frequently
quoted example of a train collision serves as a clear
illustration of how the conflict between inertia and
the molecular forces of elasticity tears asunder the
parts of the train. Thus we see that the structure—
no matter how it may have to be described exactly—
is of most decisive influence on the course of events.
It is the physicist's problem to ascertain it from the
physical effects which it produces.

After these general remarks concerning the relativity problem, I shall outline to you the history of
the ether concept briefly as follows. In the philosophy of the *Stoa*, the ether occurs first as the divine

fire spread out through the world, as the substratum
of the divine creative forces at action in the world.
One can read about the stoic ether theory, for example, in the second and third books of Cicero's work
De natura deorum (On the Nature of the Gods). In
the transition period to which Giordano Bruno belongs,
this idea mingles with the atomistic world concept
which, after its formulation in antiquity by Democritus, was taken over and developed by the Epicureans.
For Bruno the ether is an extended real entity which
permeates all bodies but is itself without limits. Here
natural science takes hold of the notion and finds in
this hypothetical medium an appropriate carrier for
the propagation of the natural forces, especially of
light, where the ordinary bodies which are perceptible
to our senses by their resistance do not suffice. With
Huygens, and also with Euler, we encounter the
light ether as a substance whose state is determined
by its density and its velocity, and which is spread
out continuously. Since it as a whole is at rest and is
excited to perform only tiny vibrations, it could at
the same time serve to provide physical reality
(hypothetical indeed) for Newton's metaphysical
notion of absolute space. But history took the opposite course. When in the nineteenth century optical
phenomena reveal themselves as part of the larger
class of electrodynamic ones, and the notion of an
electromagnetic field which no longer requires a substantial substratum is developed by Faraday and
Maxwell, the ether divests itself of its physical character, and there remains absolute space, a structural

element, which is no longer affected by matter as was the light ether. This second stage was anticipated in Newton's natural philosophy. At the beginning of his *Principia*, Newton proclaims with perfect clarity absolute space and absolute time as the entities that are *a priori* at the bottom of all laws of nature. If one asks how Newton could embrace this dogma although he adopts the empiristic program of deriving the actual run of the strata and fibers of the world according to space and time from their effects on the observable events, the answer to my mind lies chiefly in his theology, the theology of Henry More. Space is to him *sensorium Dei*, the divine omnipresence in all things. Therefore the structure of space behaves with regard to things as one would naturally imagine the behavior of an absolute God toward the world: the world is submitted to his action, but he himself is beyond the influence of any action from the world. Certainly Newton's view of the world thereby acquires a somewhat rigid and scholastic character. In his doctrine about the center of the world and the position of the sun among the fixed stars, for example, he is considerably more Aristotelian and less modern than Giordano Bruno who precedes him by more than a century. Nevertheless we must admit that the transition from the stoic ether as a deified potency of nature which is drawn into the play of the natural forces, to the geometrically rigid absolute space represents an advance of conception which is entirely in line with the transition from a mythical religion of nature to the transcendent God of Christianity.

In the third stage of the development it becomes manifest that the space-time structure is described incorrectly by the notion of absolute space; that not the state of rest but of uniform translation is an intrinsically distinguished class of motion. This recognition at the same time completely puts an end to the substantial ether. Newton himself was able to pass from uniform translation to rest only by a strange scholastic trick which shows up most peculiarly in the disposition of the *Principia* which is otherwise so rigorous. Finally, in the fourth place, the general theory of relativity permits this world structure in its inertial as well as its causal aspect again to become a physical entity which yields to the forces of matter; thus in a certain sense the circle closes, even though the quantities of condition characterizing the state of the ether have now become entirely different from those in the beginning of the development, when it appeared on the scene as a substantial medium. For this, indeed, is the fundamental physical thought underlying Einstein's general theory of relativity, that that which produces as powerful and real effects as does this structure cannot be a rigid geometric constitution of the world fixed once and for all, but is something real which not only acts upon matter but also reacts under its influence. In the dualism between inertial guidance and force, as Einstein further recognized, gravitation belongs on the side of

inertia; the suspected variability of the inertial field
and its dependence on matter manifest themselves in
the phenomena of gravitation. As seen from Newton's
philosophy, the theory of relativity thus deprives
space of its divine character. We now distinguish between the amorphous continuum and its structure:
the first retains its *a priori* character, but becomes
the counterpart of pure consciousness, while the
structural field is completely given over to the real
world and its play of forces. As a real entity it is
denoted by Einstein for good historic reasons by the
old name of the ether.

The reason why the dependence of the ether upon
matter was so hard to discern lies in the extreme predominance of the ether in its interaction with matter
—nor does the Einstein theory deny its overruling
power. If it is not a god, it is certainly a superhuman
giant. One can estimate the proportion of power to
be as $10^{20}:1$ in a sense that can be exactly specified
mathematically on the ground of the laws of nature.

If the ether were not disturbed by matter it would
abide in the condition of rest, or, speaking mathematically and more precisely, of homogeneity. In
contrast with the "spirit of unrest" that dwells in
matter, "the breast of the earth and of man," in Hölderlin's language, the ether represents the lofty,
hardly disturbed quiescence of the universe. Being of
the same essence as, and in principle on the same
plane with matter and its forces, the ether is not the
divine in nature; still we encounter in it a power
which to us human beings—who are able to produce

action only through the agent of matter—is strange, overwhelming, soothing, and before which a feeling of deep reverence is well appropriate. In this spirit the great German romantic poet Hölderlin, as late as the beginning of the nineteenth century, devoted to "Father Ether" powerful cosmic songs. And to present-day natural philosophy it is still a profound enigma, to my mind *the* deepest mystery with which it is confronted, how this powerful predominance of the ether in its interaction with matter is to be understood. What I primarily wanted to make clear to you by my exposition is how at this point age-old religious and metaphysical ideas and questions are intimately connected with the ultimate problems of actual science.

But no matter how exalted the natural power is which modern physics denotes as gravitational and inertial ether, to us who are Christians and not heathens the ether does not reveal the face of the divine ultimate essence of things. Therefore I shall now follow the line of thought which man has advanced as a second fundamental answer to the question as to the finger of God in nature: the world is not a chaos, but a *cosmos harmoniously ordered by inviolable mathematical laws.* This idea hardly has a history. We suddenly encounter it in completed form with the Pythagoreans, and from them it passes over into Platonic philosophy. Historically I should like to trace it to two sources that lie far apart. First to the age-old number-mysticism and number-magic, an inheritance of mankind from prehistoric times with which the

general lawfulness of nature, in the philosophy of
Pythagoras, the founder of the school, still appears
to have been closely bound up. The law of musical
harmony, according to which the harmonic tones are
produced by a division of the chord in integral proportions, ranks as the primal law. Following this example, one sought to reduce to integral proportions also
the evident regularity in the course of the stars, especially the planetary orbs and their periods of revolution, and called this the harmony of the spheres. Kepler ardently devoted himself to such studies and
finally wrought from them his three famous laws of
planetary motion, which inaugurated the transition
to a more profound conception of the mathematical
harmony in the laws of nature. The second source,
the anthropomorphic origin of the idea of lawful
determination in the cosmos lies in the idea of fate.
The acting ego in its existence of strife not only en-
counters the thou, the fellow man and the fellow ani-
mal, but also the resistance of a form of being essentially different from his own and towering giganti-
cally above him: earth and ocean, fire, storm and
stars. Their manifestations were first considered and
designated by language as acts, as the manifestations
of an acting being; for example, we say "The sun
shines." As soon as this primitive animism is overcome, as soon as the essential difference of external
events as contrasted with acts of the ego born out of
a cloudy mixture of insight and urge is recognized
and stressed, it appears as fate, μοίρα, "Ananke, the
compelled compulsion" (as it reads in Spitteler's
epos, *The Olympic Spring*), with the attribute of

unyielding, blind necessity, which is self-sufficient
and in no relation to any meaning. But dark ordi-
nance by fate and dark number-magic are overcome
in Greek thought by the glorious, lucid idea of mathematical lawfulness governing the world. Without
having relation to any meaning as do the acts of the
ego, the external world is thus nevertheless filled with
the light of spirit, of reason. We know in how wonderful a manner and to what extent this idea about
the structure of the external world has stood the test,
at first with regard to the motion of the stars, and
later also with regard to the confused processes on
the earth—since with Kepler and Galileo the course
of the world was reduced by an actual analysis of
nature to the changes in space-time of measurable
quantities of condition. These men succeeded in the
most difficult of all advances of the human mind—
that of subjecting speculative imagination and *a
priori* mathematical construction to reality and to
experience as it is systematically questioned in the
experiment.

In a law of nature, as we shall later establish more
precisely, simplicity is essential. "Nature loves simplicity and unity," we read in Kepler. The closely
allied category of perfection played a great part in
Aristotelian philosophy, not only as a methodical but
as an explanatory principle. Thus, according to Aristotle, the indestructibility and immutability of the
heavenly bodies asserted by him arise from their perfect spherical form. In the polemics which Galileo
directed against this conception in his dialogue on
the two principal world systems, we feel most keenly

the radical change in the interpretation of nature
that was made by Galileo. He recognizes the idea of
perfection, but he no longer seeks it in fixed forms
and individual things—here he praises mutability:
how the plant developing into a flower is something
incomparably more glorious than the crystal perfection of the bodies in the Aristotelian world, removed
from all changes. He seeks it in the dynamic connections and their lawfulness, and finds perfection no
longer an objective ultimate constituent of physical
properties, but rather a heuristic principle and a
creed conducive to research. In the evolution of Kepler's ideas this change also takes place. At the beginning he still adheres to static principles, he attempts
to discover the harmony of the planetary system in
the scheme of regular bodies. Only gradually and
laboriously does he struggle through to a more dynamic conception of the world. "Kepler, Galileo,
Bruno," says Dilthey, "share with the antique Pythagoreans the belief in a cosmos ordered according to
highest and most perfect rational mathematical laws,
and in divine reason as the origin of the rational in
nature, to which at the same time human reason is
related." On the long road of experience throughout
the following centuries, this belief has always found
new and surprising partial fulfilments in physics, the
longer the more, the most beautiful perhaps in the
Maxwell theory of the electromagnetic field. No general notion concerning the essence of the external
world can be placed parallel to this one in depth and
solidity; although we must admit that nature has

again and again proved superior to the human mind, and has forced it to abandon a preliminary conclusion, at times attempted even in a universal world law, for the sake of a deeper harmony.

It was natural for man to attribute the cause for the lawfulness of the world to the reign of souls endowed with reason. I may remind you of the words of Plato quoted at the beginning of this lecture. Kepler finds it hard to understand the obedience of the planets to his second law, which sets the velocity of the planet in functional dependence on its distance from the sun, except by assuming a planetary soul which receives within itself the image of the sun in its changing magnitude. Much more tenaciously than such a psychical interpretation has a mechanical and machinistical interpretation of the laws of nature tried to assert and maintain itself in physics. Think of Ptolemy's mechanism of wheels, think also of the multitudinous attempts to explain gravitation and all physical phenomena by the impact of hard particles. But physics has had to free itself more and more both from mechanical and psychical interpretations; in atomistic physics, this appears to have taken place only in the latest phases of development of the quantum theory. In an address given at the monument which his birthplace, Weil der Stadt, dedicated to Kepler, Eddington recently spoke of the fact that in Kepler's conception of the world, the music of the spheres was not drowned by the roar of machinery and that herein lies a deep relationship between his astronomical thinking and the development of modern physics. The harmony of the universe is neither mechanical nor psychical, it is mathematical and divine.

The Pythagoreans, and following them Plato, conceived the mathematical regularity of the cosmos merely as an order which does not bind nature or the divine in any sense other than that in which reason, for example, as an agency realizing truth, is bound by the formal logical laws. But later *Stoa* and Christianity, with their increased accentuation of the value of the individual soul, again amalgamated the idea of the cosmos with that of fate, and in the regularity of nature stressed less the order than the necessity and determination which govern relentlessly the course of all events, including human acts. With Hobbes this results in the modern positivistic determinism of which I shall have to give a more detailed discussion in the second lecture on causality.

I shall conclude this lecture with an epistemological consideration.

The beginning of all philosophical thought is the realization that the perceptual world is but an image, a vision, a phenomenon of our consciousness; our consciousness does not directly grasp a transcendental real world which is as it appears. The tension between subject and object is no doubt reflected in our conscious acts, for example, in sense perceptions. Nevertheless, from the purely epistemological point of view, no objection can be made to phenomenalism which would like to limit science to the description of what is "immediately given to consciousness." The postulation of the real ego, of the thou and of the

world, is a metaphysical matter, not judgment, but
an act of acknowledgment and belief. But this belief
is after all the soul of all knowledge. It was an error
of idealism to assume that the phenomena of consciousness guarantee the reality of the ego in an
essentially different and somehow more certain manner than the reality of the external world; in the
transition from consciousness to reality the ego, the
thou and the world rise into existence indissolubly
connected and, as it were, at one stroke.

But the one-sided metaphysical standpoint of realism is equally wrong. Viewed from it, egohood remains
a problem. Leibniz thought he had solved the conflict
between human freedom and divine predestination by
letting God (for sufficient reasons) assign existence
to certain of the infinitely many possibilities, for
example to the beings Judas and Peter, whose substantial nature then determines their entire fate. The
solution may be sufficient objectively, but it breaks
down before the desperate outcry of Judas: "Why
did *I* have to be Judas?" The impossibility of an
objective formulation of the question is evident;
therefore no answer in the form of an objective cognition can ensue. Only redemption of his soul can be
the answer. Knowledge is unable to harmonize the
luminous ego (the highest, indeed the only forum of
all cognition, truth, and responsibility) which here
asks in despair for an answer, with the dark, erring
human being that is cast out into an individual fate.
Furthermore, postulating an external world does not
guarantee that it shall constitute itself out of the
phenomena according to the cognitive work of reason

as it establishes consistency. For this to take place it is necessary that the world be governed throughout by simple elementary laws. Thus the mere postulation of the external world does not really explain what it was supposed to explain, namely, the fact that I, as a perceiving and acting being, find myself placed in such a world; the question of its reality is inseparably connected with the question of the reason for its lawful mathematical harmony. But this ultimate foundation for the ratio governing the world, we can find only in God; it is one side of the Divine Being. Thus the ultimate answer lies beyond all knowledge, in God alone; flowing down from him, consciousness, ignorant of its own origin, seizes upon itself in analytic self-penetration, suspended between subject and object, between meaning and being. The real world is not a thing founded in itself, that can in a significant manner be established as an independent existence. Recognition of the world as it comes from God cannot, as metaphysics and theology have repeatedly attempted, be achieved by cognitions crystallizing into separate judgments that have an independent meaning and assert definite facts. It can be gained only by symbolical construction. What this means will become clearer in the two following lectures.

Many people think that modern science is far removed from God. I find, on the contrary, that it is much more difficult today for the knowing person to approach God from history, from the spiritual side of the world, and from morals; for there we encounter

the suffering and evil in the world which it is difficult
to bring into harmony with an all-merciful and all-
mighty God. In this domain we have evidently not
yet succeeded in raising the veil with which our human nature covers the essence of things. But in our
knowledge of physical nature we have penetrated so
far that we can obtain a vision of the flawless harmony which is in conformity with sublime reason.
Here is neither suffering nor evil nor deficiency, but
perfection only. Nothing prevents us as scientists
from taking part in the cosmic worship that found
such powerful expression in the most glorious poem
of the German language, the song of the archangels
at the beginning of Goethe's *Faust:*

> The sun makes music as of old
> Amid the rival spheres of heaven
> On its predestined circle rolled
> With thunder speed; the angels even
> Draw strength from gazing at its glance,
> Though none its meaning fathom may:—
> The world's unwithered countenance
> Is bright as on the earliest day.

> Die Sonne tönt nach alter Weise
> In Brudersphären Wettgesang,
> Und ihre vorgeschriebne Reise
> Vollendet sie mit Donnergang.
> Ihr Anblick gibt den Engeln Stärke,
> Wenn keiner sie ergründen mag;
> Die unbegreiflich hohen Werke
> Sind herrlich wie am ersten Tag.

II

CAUSALITY

O F the various ideas which, in the first lecture, were sketched rather than developed, we wish to consider causality in somewhat greater detail. This subject is also of vital interest in the natural science of the present, since modern quantum theory has precipitated a crisis of the concept of determination which dominated science in the last centuries.

Two relatively independent components appear to me to be fused in the idea of causality. I should like to designate them for the present quite generally as *the mathematical concept of determination by law*, and *the metaphysical notion of "the reason for something,"* that is the *Bestimmungsgrund*. Somewhere Leibniz says: "Just as the inner understanding of the word 'I' unlocks the concept of substance for me, so it is the observation of my self which yields other metaphysical concepts, such as 'cause,' 'effect,' and the like." The basic intuition through which we approach the essence of causality is: I do this. In this there is no question whatever of any kind of regularity—any kind of law—which holds again and again.

Descartes brings out the decisive point in the problem of free will with particular clarity, when he demonstrates the freedom involved in the theoretical acts of affirmation and negation: When I reason that

$2+2=4$, this actual judgment is not forced upon me through blind natural causality (a view which would eliminate thinking as an act for which one can be held answerable) but something purely spiritual enters in: the circumstance that $2+2$ really equals 4, exercises a determining power over my judgment. The issue here is not that the determining factors responsible for my actions (in part) lie in me, as an existing natural being, and not outside of me; nor that entirely groundless, blind decisions are possible. But one has to acknowledge that the realm of Being, with respect to its determining factors, is not closed, but open toward mind in the ego, where meaning and being are merged in an indissoluble union. If I just now stated that the circumstance that $2+2=4$ exercises a power over my actual judgment, I did not thereby mean to imply a spiritual realm of facts or of Platonic ideas having an independent existence above reality, but I wished to emphasize that we are here dealing not with a new realm of existence but only with meaning—meaning which finds its fulfilment in reality.

The method of scientific research, primarily introduced by Galileo, presents two aspects, both equally essential, which are somewhat related to this juxtaposition of meaning and being: the *a priori* side, namely, free mathematical construction of the field of possibilities, and the *a posteriori* empirical side, the subjection of reality to experience and experiment. The history of the Renaissance shows very clearly how a positivistically inclined empiricism does

not find in itself sufficient power to push through to
a discovery of the natural law, but always sinks
back into theosophy, mysticism and magic. The approach of Leonardo and Galileo, who seek the reasons
of reality in experience, is sharply separated from
the ways of sensualistic doctrines; as the former
clearly and definitely points toward mathematical
idealism, so the latter always lead back to the primitive forms of animism; Campanella, also Cardano,
and even Bacon are examples. On the other hand,
through the great discoveries of Copernicus, Kepler,
and Galileo, as well as the accompanying theories ad-
vocating the construction of nature through *a priori*
given, logical-mathematical elements, there was established a supreme realization of the autonomy of
the human intellect and its power over matter. In the
philosophy of Descartes, which is the most universal
expression of the thought of this epoch, the new
mechanical interpretation must therefore be recon-
ciled with the idealism of freedom; for an intensified
consciousness of dignity and personal freedom resulted from that self-certainty of reason, which is so
often and so naturally bound up with the constructive power of the mathematical mind. But for rational thinking, the duality of natural determination
and personal freedom involved a serious antinomy,
since the concrete person of the individual is embedded in nature.

It is well known that the first modern theory of
determinism was carried through by Hobbes. One of
its clearest formulations we owe to Laplace. I quote

his famous words from the *Essai philosophique sur les probabilités*:

An intelligence which knows the forces acting in nature at a given instant, and the mutual positions of the natural bodies upon which they act, could, if it were furthermore sufficiently powerful to subject these data to mathematical analysis, condense into a single equation the motion of the largest heavenly bodies and of the lightest atoms; nothing would be uncertain for it, and the future as well as the past would lie open before its eyes. The human mind, in the perfection to which it has carried astronomy, offers a weak image of such an intelligence in a limited field.

If it is true that I am an existing individual performing real mental acts and at the same time a self-penetrating light, mind that is open toward meaning and reason, or, as Fichte expressed it, "force to which an eye has been lent"; and if Descartes' conviction of freedom is not deceptive—that is, if the realm of being with respect to its determining factors is not closed, but open toward reason in the ego—then this feature of openness must also manifest itself within nature and its science. Since this was not the case in natural science as it developed from Galileo's time with the native claim of embracing all of nature, this natural science became to the modern mind the power which shook the naïve belief in the independence of the ego. Everything supports the fact that living beings do not violate the exact laws of nature; I, for example, can only impart a momentum to my body by pushing off from other bodies, which thereby take on an opposite momentum. Natural science is too easily condemned as rank materialism in view of its adherence, through many centuries, to a strictly deterministic position. Anyone aware of the extensive applicability and the precision of the mathematical laws of nature, as they were revealed principally by astronomy and physics, must admit that this position was the only fruitful one; the limits of determination by law will be discovered when one follows this way to its end, not, however, by giving way to evasive compromises, out of indolence or sentimentality. We firmly believe today that we have touched these limits in quantum mechanics.

After these preliminary remarks I now turn to the problem of the determination of nature by mathematically formulated laws. I shall begin with certain epistemological considerations concerning the meaning of the law of causality. Decisive as these considerations may be for the methodology of natural science, they accomplish little, I believe, in the way of relieving the pressure which a determination through the world of things places upon the ego. In the second part, however, we shall turn to the problem proper, in order to ascertain from concrete physics, as it developed in the last decades, the character of the determination it asserts and the limits of such determination.

The transformation of the metaphysical question of cause into the scientific question of law is taught by all great scientists. The discovery of the law of falling bodies is the first important example; Galileo himself says about it in his *Discorsi:* "It does not seem to me advantageous now to examine what the cause of acceleration is." It is more important to investigate the law according to which the acceleration varies. Again, Newton says:

I have not yet been able to determine from the phenomena the cause of these properties of gravitation, and I do not invent hypotheses (*Hypotheses non fingo*). It is sufficient that gravitation exists, that it acts according to the laws we have formulated, and that it is capable of explaining all motions of heavenly bodies and of the sea. (End of *Principia.*)

Dynamics, according to the doctrines of d'Alembert and Lagrange, requires no laws which extend to the causes of physical phenomena and to the essence of such causes; it is closed in itself as a representation of the regularities of phenomena.

To be sure, the statement that the course of events is determined by means of natural laws does not exhaust the content of what appears to us, perhaps somewhat vaguely, as the relation of cause and effect. In particular, the mathematical law cannot distinguish between the determining and the determined. If several quantities a, b, c are functionally related, for example, $a+b=c$, then the value of a and b may determine that of c; but the same law may also be so construed that, by means of the quantities a and c, it determines b. If natural laws enable us to predetermine the future, we can, with their help, equally well determine the past from the present. The gen-

eral law of refraction of light in an optically inhomogeneous medium, as, for example, the atmosphere,
may, according to Snellius, be formulated as a differential law which connects the infinitesimal change
in the direction of a light ray with the change in the
velocity of propagation along the ray. But as an
alternative we may, according to Fermat, describe
the same process by reference to the principle that,
in passing from one point of the medium to a distant
point, the ray chooses that path which requires the
least time. The differential formulation corresponds
to the causal conception according to which the state
at one instant determines the change of state during
an infinitesimal interval of time; the second, the integral formulation, savors of teleology. However,
both laws are mathematically equivalent. Thus natural law is completely indifferent to causality and
finality; this difference does not concern scientific
knowledge, but metaphysical interpretation by
means of the idea of determining reason. I believe it
is necessary to state this with full clarity: the law of
nature offers as little evidence for or against a meta-
physical-teleological interpretation of the world as it
does for or against a metaphysical-causal one.

The first epistemological analysis of the law of
causality aiming to isolate that part of causality
which plays a rôle in an actual investigation of nature was undertaken by Hume. As preliminary
characteristics he finds: (1) The principle of nearby
action, according to which causally related objects
or processes must be directly connected in space-

time; the answer to the question "Why?" demands
the insertion of a continuous uninterrupted causal
chain. (2) The transition: cause → effect runs in the
time sense: past → future. (3) The necessity of the
causal bond which is commonly postulated, and
which is taken over from the idea of fate, is, according to Hume, not capable of a clear-cut empirical
interpretation. He therefore replaces necessity by
repetition and permanence; that is, whenever the
same circumstances recur, the same effect will follow
the same cause. But even with this nothing is gained,
as an event happens in its full concretion only once.
It is thus necessary that certain demands of continuity be added, stipulating that causes differing
sufficiently little from one another have effects also
differing but little; that sufficiently remote bodies or
events have a negligible effect, and so on. The phenomena must be brought under the heading of concepts; they must be united into classes determined by
typical characteristics. Thus the causal judgment,
"When I put my hand in the fire I burn myself,"
concerns a typical performance described by the
words "to put one's hand in the fire," not an individual act in which the motion of the hand and that
of the flames is determined in the minutest detail.
The causal relation therefore does not exist between
events but between types of events. First of all—and
this point does not seem to have been sufficiently
emphasized by Hume—*generally valid relations
must be isolated by decomposing the one existing
world into simple, always recurring elements.* The

formula *"dissecare naturam"* was already set up by
Bacon.

I do not intend to go into the details of an analysis of nature, but shall direct attention to only two
or three points. (1) One does not hesitate to decompose hypothetically things that are irreducible simple elements from a perceptual standpoint, as, for
example, the white sunlight into the spectral colors,
or the acceleration which the earth acquires into the
partial acceleration which the sun and the planets
separately impart to it. (2) In scientific investigation one does not stop with the perceived qualities of
a body which directly appeal to the senses, but one
introduces "concealed characters" which only manifest themselves through the reactions of that body
with others. Thus, for example, the inertial mass is
no perceivable characteristic of a body, but can only
be determined by allowing the body to react with
others and then applying the impulse law to these
reactions. This law asserts: to every isolated body a
momentum may be assigned, this momentum being a
vector with the same direction as the velocity; the
positive factor m, by which the velocity must be
multiplied in order to give the momentum, is called
the mass. If several bodies react on each other, the
sum of their momenta after the reaction is the same
as before. It is only through this law that the concept of momentum, and with it that of mass, attains a
definite content; separated from it they are simply
suspended in the air. It is this constructive method
alone which permitted natural science to penetrate

beyond the narrow bounds of the purely geometrical concepts, within which Descartes attempted to confine it. Even the geometrical concepts have essentially this constructive character. (3) It is typical of the mathematizing sciences (in contradistinction to the descriptive ones) that they pass from the classification of given examples, like Linnaeus' classification of the actually occurring plants, to the ideal, constructive generation of the possible. Instead of classifying the perceivable colors, physics sets up the concept of ether waves, which may differ only in direction and wave length. Both direction and wave length, however, vary within a predetermined domain of possibilities. Thus the four-dimensional medium of space and time is the field of possible coincidences of events. Such a field, and a most important one, open to our free construction, is the continuum of numbers. To be sure, the analysis must be carried to the point where each element may be determined, in its full concretion, through particular values of such constructive moments as direction and wave length, which vary within a domain completely surveyable since it arises from free construction. The law of causality then maintains that between such quantitative elements there exist universally valid, simple, exact, functional relations.

Let us now pass from elementary analysis to the idea of natural law. Is it so self-evident that it requires no further exposition? I think not. Above all I wish here to emphasize two points.

The assertion that nature is governed by strict

laws is devoid of all content if we do not add the
statement that it is governed by mathematically simple laws. This matter is somewhat analogous to the
fundamental law of multiple proportions in chemis-
try: it loses all its content unless we add that the
combination occurs in small integral multiples of the
relative atomic weights. That the notion of law becomes empty when an arbitrary complication is permitted was already pointed out by Leibniz in his
Metaphysical Treatise. Thus simplicity becomes a
working principle in the natural sciences. If a set of
observations giving the dependence of a quantity y
on a quantity x lie on a straight line when plotted,
we anticipate, on account of the mathematical simplicity of the straight line, that it will represent the
exact law of dependence; we are then able to ex-
trapolate and make predictions. One cannot help but
admit that this working principle of simplicity has
stood the test well. Euclidean geometry, for example,
as a science concerning the metric behavior of rigid
bodies, was gained from very rough experiences as
their simplest interpretation. In later precise geometrical and astronomical measurements this geometry proved to hold much more exactly than we could
have anticipated from its origin. Analogous cases
are continually encountered in physics. The aston-
ishing thing is not that there exist natural laws, but
that the further the analysis proceeds, the finer the
details, the finer the elements to which the phenomena are reduced, the simpler—and not the more complicated, as one would originally expect—the fun-

damental relations become and the more exactly do they describe the actual occurrences. But this circumstance is apt to weaken the metaphysical power of determinism, since it makes the meaning of natural law depend on the fluctuating distinction between mathematically simple and complicated functions or classes of functions.

In the same direction points the epistemological observation that the principle, "under the same circumstances the same results will follow" (no matter how one may interpret it), does not hold as something verifiable by experience. An inductive proof of the proposition, as Helmholtz says, would be very shaky; the degree of validity would at best be comparable with that of the meteorological rules. It is rather a norm whose validity we enforce in building up our experience. This is well illustrated by the example of the spectral analysis of white light by means of a prism, to which we referred previously. In obvious contradiction to the fundamental proposition that under equal circumstances equal causes will call forth equal reactions, two colors which appear as the same white to the senses yield totally different spectra, in general, after passing through the same prism. In order to save our fundamental proposition we invent a "hidden" variety in white light, which is most suitably described by giving the spectrum itself with its intensity of distribution; it is for this reason that we are led, in physics, to regard simple white light as a composite of colors. (We note that here at first the apparatus used in the reaction, the prism with its special properties, still plays a rôle; it is only after varying the shape, substance, and orientation of the prism with respect to the light rays, and thus separating the two influences from one another, that one arrives at a scale of wave lengths which is independent of the prism.)

Constructive natural science is confronted with the general problem of assigning to objects such constructive characteristics that their behavior under circumstances described by the same kind of characteristics is entirely determined and predictable by means of the natural laws. The implicit definition of the characteristics is bound to these laws. The fact that we do not find but enforce the general principles of natural knowledge was particularly emphasized by the conventionalism of H. Poincaré. But I believe one may also consider the hastily sketched developments just completed as an interpretation of Kant's doctrine of the categories.

These considerations force upon us the impression that the law of causality as a principle of natural science is one incapable of formulation in a few words, and is not a self-contained exact law. Its content can in fact only be made clear in connection with a complete phenomenological description of how reality constitutes itself from the immediate data of consciousness. Kant's naïve formulation: "Everything that happens (comes into existence) implies something from which it follows according to a rule," can hardly satisfy us any longer. At the same time "fate" as expressed in the natural laws appears to be so weakened by our analysis that only through misunderstanding can it be placed in opposition to free will.

True as this may be with respect to the general principle of causality, as a methodical principle of natural science, yet I believe that this epistemological subterfuge, so eagerly adopted by just the deeper thinkers, is invalidated by concrete physics itself. So far we have spoken only of the methodology of natural science and its leading principles. But through it results concrete physics itself, deeply rooted in the fertile soil of experience. Perhaps there is no strict logical way leading from the facts to our theories; but physics as a whole is convincing for everyone who devotes himself seriously to an investigation of the cosmos. It is now no longer a question of the general idea of the mathematically simple natural law, but the definite concrete laws of nature themselves stand before us in their wonderfully transparent mathematical harmony. The previous decomposition of the world into individual systems, individual events and their elements vanishes more and more as the theoretical structure is completed; the world appears again as a whole, with all its parts interactively bound to one another. The development tends distinctly toward a unified, all-embracing world law. In the actually known natural law lies a restriction of the world structure which in all metaphysical seriousness sets a limit even to the claims of autonomy of the mind. Therefore we shall now concern ourselves with this lawfulness itself, to see how it is constituted and where its limits are.

A first consideration is this: physics has never given support to that truly consistent determinism which maintains the unconditioned necessity of everything which happens. Even from its most extreme standpoints, including Newton's physics of central forces as well as modern field-theory, physics always supposed the state of the world at a certain moment in a section $t=$const. to be arbitrary and unrestricted by laws. Even in Laplace's universe there was an "open place" which could be chosen at random among the sections $t=$const. of the world. This perhaps suffices to reconcile mechanical necessity with Divine Predestination. Descartes argues thus: since neither the nature nor the distribution of the material constituents of the world nor their initial velocities are to be derived by pure reasoning, God could have set up the natural order in innumerable ways; He chose one to suit His purpose. Newton makes similar remarks in the conclusion of his *Optics*. But this degree of arbitrariness seems to me insufficient to admit human free will. My own destiny in the world from birth to death could still, on this view, be fixed by the state of the world in a time-section which has no contact with my existence, with the world-line of my life, since it precedes or follows it. Hence Kant's solution of the dilemma (the meaning of which was so vague even to himself that he found difficulties in understanding the changes of human character) can only be carried through hon-

estly if one believes in the existence of the individual
from eternity to eternity, in the form of a Leibniz
monad, say, or by metempsychosis as the Indians and
Schopenhauer believe. Nevertheless, it is of sufficient
importance that physics has always admitted a loop-
hole in the necessity of Nature.

The antinomy between freedom and determination
takes its most acute form in the relation between
knowing and being. Let us assume once more with
Laplace that the state of the world at one moment,
i.e., a three-dimensional section $t=$const., defines by
strict mathematical laws its course during all past
and future time. Then we might suppose that I can
calculate the future from what I know (or can know)
here and now at the world point O. I should like to
state with all emphasis that this antinomy, which formerly existed, disappears in the relativity theory. In
the first lecture I described the causal structure according to which a kind of conical surface issues from
each point O of the four-dimensional world as vertex
and separates the causal past and future. Causality
is here not merely a methodological principle but becomes through this structure an objective constituent of the world. In the figure the section $t=$const.
through O separates the past and the future sheets
of the cone through O. But it is not this plane section, it is the surface of the backward light-cone
which separates what is knowable at O from what is
not. And it is a mathematical consequence of the classical physical laws that whereas the backward half of
the world, cut off by $t=$const., determines the whole,
the interior of the backward light-cone does not.

That is to say, only after a deed is done can I know all its causal premises.

If we regard, however, our problem as concerning reality alone and not concerning the relation of knowledge and reality, and if free action shall be possible in this real world, then we must demand that the content of the forward pointing cone through O shall not be completely determined by the rest of the world. This would contradict classical physics. But classical physics, after decades of invasion by statistical theories, is now finally superseded by the quantum theory, and a new situation has arisen.

In three grams of hydrogen there are about 10^{24} hydrogen molecules whirling about; it is of course impossible to calculate exactly their motion under the forces they experience from the walls of the container and from one another. Their average velocity determines the temperature, their bombardment of the walls, or rather the impulse per unit area it conveys, the pressure. Certain mean values are what our observations measure and these can be predicted by probability calculations, without detailed investigation of the motion. Consider, for example, a cubical container divided up into many small cubes, all of equal size, and suppose the chance of a given molecule to be in one of these is the same for each and that the space probabilities of the different molecules are independent in the statistical sense. Then we can show that the gas density in each of the small cubes differs with utterly overwhelming probability by less than, say, .01% from the mean density of the whole. Macroscopically speaking, the gas in equilib-

rium is uniformly dense. In the same way the kinetic
theory of gases, first formulated by Daniel Ber-
noulli, leads to the other well-known gas laws.

The theory of probability not only tells us the
mean value of a quantity, but also how great its
deviation from this mean may be expected to be. The
spontaneous variations in the density of the atmosphere which arise through the random motions of
its molecules are the cause of the diffusion of the
sun's rays in daylight, which makes a cloudless sky
appear not black but blue. Small though they are
individually, combined they produce a perceptible
effect. Such variation-phenomena are the main supports of the statistical theory. The powerful re-
searches of Maxwell and Boltzmann have made clear
that the majority of physical concepts are not exact
in the sense of classical physics, but statistical mean
values, with a certain degree of indetermination, and
that most of the familiar laws of physics, especially
all those which concern the thermodynamics of
atomic matter, are not to be regarded as strictly
valid natural laws but as statistical regularities.

The first epistemological attitude toward statistical physics was to regard the probability theory simply as a short cut to certain consequences of the
exact laws. For instance, strictly speaking, one
would have to prove by means of the classical laws
of motion that the time intervals during which the
gas deviates noticeably from thermodynamic equilib-
rium were together vanishingly small as compared to
the whole period of observation. Attempts at such
proofs were indeed made, but it was always necessary

to introduce an unproved hypothesis, the so-called ergodic hypothesis, at the critical point. If we adhere to the actual practice of physical research we are bound to admit that with the progress of the statistical theory and its continual increase in fruitfulness the attempts to base it on strict functional laws have gradually been abandoned. Historical evolution has spoken and demands that we recognize statistical concepts as equally fundamental with the concepts of law. I believe that such historical evolution can exert a more compelling pressure than any reasoning which pretends to be heaven knows how rigorous.

It should be remarked in this connection that in the world of exact laws time is reversible; changing t into $-t$ makes no difference. On the other hand, the definite direction of flow from past to future is perhaps the one outstanding mark of subjective time. This uniqueness of direction enters into physics not through its functional laws, but through our probability judgments; from a state at a given moment we deduce the probable state at a subsequent moment according to computed probabilities, and not the state at a previous one. Thus probability exposes a part of the causal idea which was quite suppressed in the exact laws.

Yet only the latest aspect of physics, quantum mechanics, has reduced the statistical nature of physical lawfulness to its ultimate foundations. This step became necessary in order to give an account of the double nature of physical entities, brought into evidence first in the case of light. Light is a spatially continuous undulatory process of electromagnetic nature. Only this conception enables us to understand diffraction and interference. But on the other hand a number of phenomena discovered in the last decades force us to conceive of light as consisting of single quanta, thrown out from the source of light in definite directions, and whose energy content is determined by the frequency, or the color of the light. I will describe here one of these phenomena. If a plate of metal is irradiated with ultra-violet light, electrons are emitted from the plate. Assuming the intensity of the light to be small, the energy of the wave which traverses an atom would not suffice to remove an electron from the atomic system. Even if we imagine some kind of a mechanism allowing the accumulation of wave energy within the atom, this effect could only begin after a long period of accumulation. Instead of this, it sets in immediately. The force with which the electrons are knocked out is totally independent of the intensity of the light; but it depends on its color. Only the number of electrons emitted in unit time increases with the intensity. This process can only be understood if light consists of single quanta. The energy content of such a light quantum, which hits an atom, is carried over to an electron, thus enabling this electron to break its bond with the nucleus of the atom, and furthermore imparting to the electron a certain kinetic energy. This energy depends on the energy content of the light quantum and hence on the color of the light. The dual nature of light—its being a wave capable of interference and also at the same time a light quantum striking suddenly here and there—we try to cover by assuming that the intensity of the wave field at a certain point represents the relative probability that a light quantum will be at that point. The more intense the light, the denser the accumulation of light quanta in unit time. The wave field obeys a strict functional law. But exactly the same condition prevails for the constituents of matter, the electrons. Everyday experiences suggest that their nature is corpuscular. But electrons have lately been shown to be susceptible of diffraction and interference. Hence there exist precise laws, but they deal with wave fields and therefore with quantities, which for real events have only the significance of probabilities. They determine the actual processes in the same way that a priori probabilities determine statistical mean values, frequencies—always containing a factor of uncertainty.

You know how it is possible with the aid of a prism or a grating to select monochromatic light from natural light. All light quanta in a ray of monochromatic light have the same definite energy and the same momentum. If we let the ray traverse a Nicol prism, we impress on it a certain direction of polarization. Let us describe this in terms of light quanta. A certain light quantum either will pass through the Nicol or it will not; hence there may be ascribed to the light quantum a certain quantity q_s corresponding to the position s of the Nicol, and taking on the values $+1$ or -1, according as the light quantum passes through or not. The monochromatic, polarized, plane light wave is the utmost in homogeneity that is obtainable. But we observe that such a homogeneous ray of light is again split up into a transmitted and reflected ray, when sent through a second Nicol in a position t different from s. The relative intensities are completely determined by the angle between the two positions s and t. They represent the probabilities that for a light quantum with $q_s=1$, the quantity $q_t= +1$ or -1. The ray of light which passed through both Nicols is not more homogeneous than the ray which passed through only the first one: it is of exactly the same character as it would have been if we had omitted the first Nicol. Hence the selection due to the first Nicol is destroyed by the second one. It is legitimate to speak of the quantity q_s for a light quantum, because there exists a method of determining its value. We can also speak of the quantity q_t. But it is meaningless to ask for the values taken simultaneously by the quantities q_s, q_t for a light quantum, because measuring q_t by selecting the light quanta with $q_t=1$ destroys the possibility of measuring q_s by selecting the light quanta with $q_s=1$.

This impossibility is not due to human limitation, but must be regarded as an essential one. Another example will make this clearer. An atom of silver possesses a certain magnetic moment, it is a small magnet of definite strength and direction. It can be represented by an arrow, the vector of magnetic moment. This vector has, in any spatial direction z, a component m_z, capable of taking on only two values, ± 1, when measured in a certain unit, the magneton. By means of a magnetic field inhomogeneous in the direction z, it is possible to separate from a beam of atoms flying through the field the two component beams for which m_z equals $+1$ and -1 respectively. The same evidently applies in any other spatial direction. But a vector, whose components in every spatial direction are capable of taking on only the values ± 1, is geometrically absurd. The resolution of this paradox is this: if the component m_z is fixed by the separation, then no further component can be determined. Only probabilities can be calculated for their possible values ± 1.

Classical physics in attempting to establish conditions which would guarantee maximum homogeneity, assumed that for such a "pure case" any physical quantity of the physical system considered took on a well defined value, which under the same conditions would always be reproduced. Quantum mechanics also requires the experimenter to create a pure case whose homogeneity cannot be increased. But the ideal of classical physics is not realizable for quantum mechanics. We must not ask what value is taken on by a physical quantity in a certain pure case, but instead what the probability is that this physical quantity will take on a given value in this pure case. The idea that an electron describes a path cannot be upheld any longer. It is true that an electron's position at a certain instant can be measured; its velocity, too, is measurable, but not both at the same time. The measurement of position destroys the possibility of an exact measurement of speed. There is no human incapacity involved; the difficulty lies in the very nature of things. The meaning of a physical quantity is bound to the method by which it is measured. The attributes with which physics deals manifest themselves only through experiments and reactions which are based on postulated laws of nature. Formerly physicists took the point of view that these attributes were assigned to the physical bodies themselves, independently of whether or not the measurements necessary to establish them were actually carried out. It was proper to connect them by the logical "and"; it was reasonable to postulate determinism and to satisfy this methodical postulate by introducing suitably chosen, concealed attributes. This epistemological position of constructive science is now submitted to an essential restriction in quantum mechanics.

We may try to escape this verdict by saying that the wave field, which obeys precise laws, is reality. Nevertheless it is a fact that this wave field cannot be observed directly, but only determines all observable quantities in the same way that *a priori* probabilities determine statistical frequencies. In this connection the uncertainty principle is unavoidable. We may say that there exists a world, causally closed and controlled by precise laws, but in order that I, the observing person, may come in contact with its actual existence, it must open itself to me. The connection between that abstract world beyond and the one which I directly perceive is necessarily of a statistical nature. This fact, together with the new insight which modern physics affords into the relation between subject and object, opens several ways of reconciling personal freedom with natural law. It would be premature, however, to propose a definite and complete solution of the problem. One of the great differences between the scientist and the impatient philosopher is that the scientist bides his time. We must await the further development of science, perhaps for centuries, perhaps for thousands of years, before we can design a true and detailed picture of the interwoven texture of Matter, Life and Soul. But the old classical determinism of Hobbes and Laplace need not oppress us any longer.

Another feature of quantum mechanics is worth mentioning. The state of a physical system is determined when for each physical quantity of the system the probability of its taking on each possible value is known. It is true therefore that the state of a system consisting of two electrons determines the states of both electrons, but the converse does not follow. The knowledge of the states of the two parts of a system by no means fixes the state of the whole system. We find here a definite and far-reaching verification of the principle that the whole is more than the sum of its parts. Modern vitalism, among whose proponents I mention first of all Driesch, has attempted to reduce the independence of life, its essential distinction from non-organic processes, to the concepts of Gestalt or the Whole. According to vitalism the living organism reacts as a whole; its functions are not additive. The manner in which its structure is preserved throughout growth, in spite of all outside influences and perturbations, is not to be explained by small scale causal reactions between the elementary parts of the organism. Now we see that according to quantum physics the same applies even to inorganic nature and is not peculiar to organic processes. It is out of the question to derive the state of the whole from the state of its parts. This leads to conditions which may most plainly if not most correctly be interpreted as a peculiar non-causal "understanding" between the elementary particles, that is prior to and independent of the control exercised by differential laws which regulate probabilities. The rule of W. Pauli that two electrons may never be found in the same quantum state is one of the best illustrations. It seems therefore that the quantum theory is called upon to bridge the gap between inorganic and organic nature; to join them in the sense of placing the origin of those phenomena which confront us in the fully developed organism as Life, Soul and Will back in the same original order of nature to which atoms and electrons also are subject. So today less than ever do we need to doubt the objective unity of the whole of nature, less than ever to despair of attaining unity of method in all natural sciences.

III

INFINITY

IN the first lecture I pointed out that the Greeks made the divergence between the finite and the infinite fruitful for the understanding of reality, and that this is one of their greatest achievements. To illustrate how the early Greek thinkers formulated the notion of the infinite in a manner enabling it to bear upon science, I shall start with a fragment transmitted to us from Anaxagoras: "In the small there is no smallest, but there is always still a smaller. For what is can never cease to exist through division, no matter how far this process be pursued." This statement, of course, refers to space or a body. The continuum, Anaxagoras says, cannot be composed of discrete elements which are "chopped off from one another, as it were, with a hatchet." Space is not only infinite in the sense that in it one nowhere reaches an end; but at every place it is infinite if one proceeds inward toward the small. A point can only be identified more and more precisely by the successive stages of a process of division continued *ad infinitum*. This is in contrast with the state of immobile and completed being in which space appears to direct perception. For the *quale* filling it, space is the principle of distinction which primally creates the possibility for a diverseness of qualitative character; but space is at the same time distinction

and contact, continuous connection, so that no piece
can be "chopped off . . . with a hatchet." Hence a
real spatial thing can never be given adequately; it
unfolds its "inner horizon" in an infinite process of
continually new and more precise experiences. Consequently it appears impossible to postulate a real
thing as being, as closed and complete in itself. In
this manner the problem of the continuum becomes
the motive for an epistemological idealism: Leibniz,
among others, testifies that it was the search for a
way out of the "labyrinth of the continuum" which
first led him to conceive of space and time as orders
of the phenomena. "From the fact that a body cannot be decomposed mathematically into primal elements," he says, "it follows immediately that it is
nothing substantial but only an ideal construction
designating merely a possibility of parts, but by no
means anything real."

Anaxagoras is opposed by the strictly atomistic
theory of Democritus. One of his arguments against
the unlimited divisibility of bodies is approximately
as follows: "It is contended that division is possible;
very well, let it be performed. What remains? No
bodies; for these could be divided still further, and
the division would not have progressed to the ultimate stage. There could only be points, and the body
would have to be composed of points, which is evidently absurd." The impossibility of conceiving the
continuum as in a stage of rigid being cannot be
illustrated more pregnantly than by Zeno's familiar
paradox about the race of Achilles with the tortoise.

The tortoise has a start of length 1; if Achilles moves with twice the speed of the tortoise, the tortoise will be the distance $\frac{1}{2}$ ahead of him at the moment when Achilles arrives at its starting point. When Achilles has covered this distance also, the tortoise will have completed a path of length $\frac{1}{4}$, and so on, *ad infinitum;* whence it is to be concluded that the swift-footed Achilles never catches up with the reptile. The

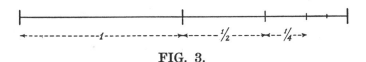

FIG. 3.

observation that the successive partial sums of the series

$$1 + \tfrac{1}{2} + \tfrac{1}{4} + \cdot \cdot \cdot$$

do not grow beyond all bounds but converge toward 2, by means of which the paradox is thought to be done away with today, is certainly important, pertinent and elucidating. But if the distance of length 2 really consists of infinitely many partial distances of length 1, $\frac{1}{2}$, $\frac{1}{4}$, . . . as "chopped off" integral parts, then it contradicts the essence of the infinite, the "incompletable," to say that Achilles has finally run through them all. Aristotle remarks with reference to the solution of Zeno's paradox, that "the moving does not move by counting," or more precisely:

If the continuous line is divided into two halves, the one dividing point is taken for two; it is both beginning and

end. But as one divides in this manner, neither the line nor
the motion are any longer continuous. . . . In the continuous there is indeed an unlimited number of halves, but only
in possibility, not in reality.

Since Leibniz seeks the foundation of the phenomena in a world of absolute substances, he has to ac-
cept the stringent argumentation of Democritus; he
conceives the idea of the monad. He says, in agreement with Aristotle:

In the ideal or the continuum the whole precedes the parts.
. . . Here the parts are only potential. But in substantial
things the simple precedes the aggregates, and the parts are
given actually and before the whole. These considerations
resolve the difficulties concerning the continuum, difficulties
that arise only if one considers the continuum as something
real which in itself has real parts prior to any division performed by us, and if one regards matter as a substance.

This suggests, as a solution of the antinomy of
the continuum, the distinction between actuality and
potentiality, between being and possibility. The ap-
plication of mathematical construction to reality
then ultimately rests on the double nature of reality,
its subjective and objective aspect: that reality is
not a thing in itself, but a thing appearing to a
mental ego. If we assume Plato's metaphysical doctrine and let the image appearing to consciousness
result from the concurrence of a "motion" issuing
partly from the ego and partly from the object, then
extension, the perceptual form of space and time as
the qualitatively undifferentiated field of free possi-

bilities, must be placed on the side of the ego. Mathematics is not the rigid and uninspiring schematism which the layman is so apt to see in it; on the contrary, we stand in mathematics precisely at that point of intersection of limitation and freedom which is the essence of man himself.

If now we proceed to formulate these old ideas a little more precisely, we first discover the infinite in a form more primitive than that of the continuum, namely in the sequence of natural numbers 1, 2, 3, . . .; and only with their help can we begin to attack the problem of the mathematical description of the continuum. Four stages can be distinguished in the development of arithmetic as regards the part played by the infinite. The first stage is characterized by individual concrete judgments, like $2 < 3$, the number symbol $//$ is contained in the symbol $///$. In the second stage there appears, for example, the idea of $<$, of "being contained" for arbitrary number symbols; and also the proposition of hypothetic generality: if any two number symbols a, b, are given, either $a = b$, or $a < b$, or $b < a$. The domain of the actually given is hereby not transgressed, since the assertion purports to be valid only when definite numbers are given. Something entirely new, however, takes place in the third stage, when I embed the actually occurring number symbols in the sequence of all possible numbers, which originates by means of a generating process in accordance with the principle that from a given number n a new one, the following one n', can always be generated. Here being is projected onto the background of the possible, or more precisely into an ordered manifold of possibilities producible according to a fixed procedure and open into infinity. Methodically this standpoint finds its expression in the definition and conclusion by complete induction. The principle of complete induction states that in order to establish that a property P relating to an arbitrary natural number n belongs to every such number, it is sufficient to prove: (α) 1 has the property P; (β) if n is any number having the property P, the following number n' also has the property P. The familiar method of distinguishing the even and the odd numbers from one another by "counting off two at a time" is a simple example of the definition by complete induction; it can be put in the form: (α) 1 is odd; (β) according as n is even or odd, n' is odd or even.

At this stage, the general statements of the science of numbers deal with the freedom of bringing the sequence of numbers to a stop at an arbitrary place. This consummates the transition to theoretical cognition proper: the transition from the *a posteriori* description of the actually given to the *a priori* construction of the possible. The given is embedded in the ordered manifold of the possible, not on the basis of descriptive characteristics, but on the basis of certain mental or physical operations and reactions to be performed on it—as, for example, the process of counting. The fourth stage of arithmetic will not be discussed in detail until later. It is the stage in which, following the prototype of the Platonic doctrine of ideas, the possible is converted into transcendental and absolute being, in its totality naturally inaccessible to our intuition.

For the moment we refrain from taking this dangerous step and turn from the natural numbers to the continuum, asking how it must be described as the substratum of possible divisions which are continued *ad infinitum*. As an example I take the one-dimensional segment. I divide it into two pieces by a point (division of the first stage); in the second stage of division each of them is again decomposed into two pieces by a dividing point, so that we now have four pieces. In the division of the third stage, each of them is again divided into two, and so on, *ad infinitum*. At every step of the division, the number of pieces rises to twice its previous value; after the nth stage of division it amounts to 2^n. This is the method of diaeresis by means of which Plato attempted to build up his ideal numbers. In the succession of divisions of the first, second, third, . . . nth, . . . stage, we encounter the developing infinite sequence of numbers. I should like to prescribe that

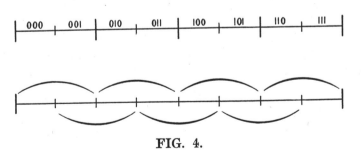

FIG. 4.

the division shall always be a bisection. But as long as I adhere to the intuitive nature of the continuum, I am prohibited from doing so; while by its very nature the continuum is divisible, the limits of the division can never be set exactly, although there is the possibility of improving the exactness and fineness of the division by continuing it to higher stages indefinitely. Hence we can at first set the limits only with a certain vagueness, but we must imagine that as we progress to the more advanced stages of the division, the division points of the preceding stages are fixed more and more precisely. Here we have to do with a process of "becoming" which in a really given continuum can only be performed up to a certain stage. But from the performance of this process on a concrete continuum, we can abstract its arithmetic scheme, and this is determined into infinity; this scheme is the subject matter of the mathematical theory of the continuum. In order to describe the arithmetic structure of the division, one must characterize the successively formed pieces in a systematic manner by symbols and indicate by means of these symbols how the pieces of the nth division stage adjoin, and how these pieces are formed from those of the preceding stage by the nth division. If the left half is always characterized by 0 and the right half by 1, the following divisional scheme is obtained:

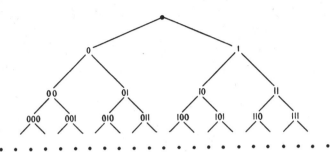

FIG. 5.

One can also consider the simple sequence of natural numbers as such a scheme of division: here an undivided entity is decomposed in one piece (the 1) which is retained as a unit, and an undivided remainder; the remainder is again decomposed in one piece (2) and an undivided remainder, and so on. The most illustrative realization of this process is time, as it is open into the future and again and again a fragment of it is lived through. Here not every part but only the last remainder is always subjected to bipartition. This is a simpler divisional scheme than that of the continuum, yet in principle it is of the same kind.

We combine every two adjacent parts of the nth stage to form a dual interval of the nth stage. (See Fig. 4.) These intervals overlap in such a manner that if a point is known with sufficient accuracy, one can with certainty indicate one of the dual intervals of the nth stage in which it falls. An individual place is thus fixed more and more precisely, caught by an infinite sequence of dual intervals each of which lies entirely within the preceding one. This process is in principle equivalent to the one taught by Eudoxos in antiquity and used to locate points in the continuum and to distinguish them from one another. What modern times have added is the recognition of the fact that the sequence must not be considered only as a means for describing the location of a given point the existence of which is secured independently, but that it originally generates the point in the continuum constructively. Every such sequence furnishes a point, and in the arithmetic scheme the points are created by this procedure. It is only on the basis of this constructive turn that a mathematical mastery, an analysis, of continuity is possible.

But there is still a problem in the idea of the infinite sequence. All essential features of our analysis are preserved and the conditions are a little easier to describe if we take as its basis the sequence of natural numbers instead of the scheme of continued bisection. A sequence of natural numbers is being formed if I arbitrarily choose a first number, then a second, a third, and so forth: "free sequence of choice." But statements concerning this sequence have meaning only if their truth can be decided at a finite stage of the development. For example, we may ask if the number 1 occurs among the numbers of the sequence up to the 10th stage, but not whether 1 occurs at all, since the sequence never reaches completion. An individual definite sequence, determined into infinity, cannot be produced in this way through definite choice, but a law is necessary which allows us to calculate in general from the arbitrary natural number n the number occurring at the nth place of the sequence. If one adheres to this scheme, one sees that in agreement with a remark of Aristotle quoted above it is quite impossible to decompose the continuous segment $0 \ldots 1$ into two parts $0 \ldots \frac{1}{2}, \frac{1}{2} \ldots 1$ in such a manner that every point x belongs to either the one or the other of the two halves.

We have now dealt with the infinite in two forms: (1) the free possibility of bringing the sequence of numbers $1, 2, 3, \ldots$ to a stop at an arbitrary place (single act of choice); (2) the free possibility of forming a continually developing and never ending sequence of natural numbers (act of choice repeated ad infinitum), which, however, turns into a law when it is to represent a special sequence determined into infinity.

Before the discovery of the irrational by Pythagoras or the mathematicians of the Pythagorean school, as long as only fractions had been used in measuring segments, the opinion prevailed that an individual point in the continuum could be fixed by one or two natural numbers, numerator and denominator of a fraction; the infinite (2) was thereby reduced to (1). But that would mean that an arbitrary sequence of numbers $\mathcal{L}$ would by a lawful rule determine a natural number $n_{\mathcal{L}}$, which characterizes the sequence itself in a unique way like a name. This is evidently impossible. The name $n_{\mathcal{L}}$ must be determined when the development of the sequence $\mathcal{L}$ has reached a certain place. It would not have to be a fixed place that can be indicated in advance, for example the 2d or the 100,000th, but could depend on the outcome of the acts of choice; eventually, however, $n_\mathcal{L}$ must be fixed and then cannot be altered by the further development of the sequence. But then all sequences having the same beginning up to this place furnish the same $n_\mathcal{L}$, no matter how they may differ from one another in their further development.

In this exposition I have so far largely followed the Dutch mathematician Brouwer who has in our day rigorously followed out the intuitional standpoint in mathematics. This standpoint emphasizes the conflict between being and possibility. Metaphysics has at all times tried to overcome the dualism between subject and object, being and possibility, existence and meaning, limitation and freedom. At the end of the first lecture, I expressed my conviction that the origin and the reconciliation of this divergence can lie only in God. The attempt presented by realism to elevate the object to the dignity of absolute being was doomed to fail from the start; as was also the opposite attempt of idealism to endow the subject with the same high independence. In mathematics also, partly through its dependence on philosophy, the inclination toward the absolute which is evidently deeply rooted in man has asserted itself. Having described the infinite in mathematics under the category of possibility in the first part of my lecture, I want now to discuss the

attempts to convert the field of possibilities that is
open into infinity into a closed domain of absolute
existence. Four different attempts to reach this goal
stand out in the course of history. The two older
ones really have to do with the continuum only.

The first and most radical attempt makes the continuum consist of countable discrete elements, atoms.
This procedure was followed already in antiquity by
Democritus in explaining the nature of matter, and
has met with most brilliant success in modern physics. Plato, clearly conscious of his proposed goal—
the salvation of the phenomenon through the idea,
seems to have been the first to conceive a consistent
atomism of space. The atomistic theory of space was
renewed in Islamic philosophy by the Mutakallimun,
in the Occident by Giordano Bruno's doctrine of the
minimum. Revived by the quantum theory this idea
reappears in our time in discussions about the foundations of physics. But so far it has always remained
pure speculation and has never found the least contact with reality.

The second attempt deals with the infinitely small.
The tangent to a curve at the point P is considered
as the line joining P to the infinitely neighboring
point of the curve, not as the limiting position which
the secant $P\,Q$ approaches indefinitely as the point
Q converges toward P along the curve; velocity is
the quotient of the infinitely small segment described
in the infinitely small time dt, divided by dt, not the
limit to which the corresponding quotient formed for
a finite time interval converges when one lets the
length of the time interval decrease below every

bound. Galileo compares the bending of a line into a regular polygon of a thousand sides with winding it on a circle; he considers this actually equivalent to the bending of the line into a polygon of infinitely many, infinitely small sides, although the individual sides cannot be separated from one another. Condensation and rarefaction of matter are interpreted by him as an intermixing of infinitely small filled and empty parts of space in changing proportions. Although Eudoxos had rejected the infinitely small by means of a rigorously formulated axiom, this idea, vague and incomprehensible, becomes in the eighteenth century the foundation of infinitesimal calculus. The founders themselves, Newton and Leibniz, expressed with some degree of clarity the correct conception that this calculus does not deal with a fixed infinitely small quantity but a transition toward the limit zero; but this conception is not the guiding principle in the subsequent development of their ideas, and they evidently ignore the fact that the limiting process not only has to determine the value of the limit, but must first guarantee its existence. For this reason modern infinitesimal calculus cannot for centuries compare with the Greek theory of the continuum as regards logical rigor. But on the other hand it has widened the range of problems for it attacks from the very first the analysis of arbitrary continuous forms and processes, especially processes of motion. In our cultural sphere the passionate urge toward reality is more powerful than is the clear-sighted Greek *ratio*.

The limiting process finally won the victory, and

thereby this second attempt to transfix the becoming continuum into rigid being had also failed. For the limit is an inevitable notion the importance of which is not affected by our accepting or rejecting the infinitely small. And once it has been conceived, it is seen to make the infinitely small superfluous. Infinitesimal analysis purports to derive the behavior of the finite from the behavior of the infinitely small, the latter being governed by elementary laws; so, for example, it deduces from the universal law of attraction for two material "volume elements" the magnitude of the attraction of arbitrarily shaped, extended bodies with homogeneous or non-homogeneous mass distribution. But if one does not here interpret the infinitely small "potentially" in the sense of the limiting process, the one has nothing to do with the other, their behaviors, the one in the domain of the finite and the other in the domain of the infinitely small, become entirely independent of one another, and the connecting link is broken. Here Eudoxos' view was doubtless correct.

At first it may seem as though this victory of the limiting process ultimately realized Aristotle's doctrine that the infinite exists only δυνάμει, in potentiality, in the state of becoming and ceasing to be, but not ἐνέργεια. This is far from true! The efforts to establish the foundation of analysis in the nineteenth century from Cauchy to Weierstrass, which start out from the limit notion, result in a new, powerful attempt to overcome the dynamics of the infinite in favor of static concepts: the theory of sets. The individual convergent sequence, such as, for example, the sequence of the partial sums of the Leibniz series $\frac{1}{1} - \frac{1}{3} + \frac{1}{5} - \frac{1}{7} + \cdot \cdot \cdot$, which converges toward $\frac{\pi}{4}$, does not develop according to a lawless process to which we have to intrust ourselves blindly in order to find out what it produces from step to step; instead it is fixed once and for all by a definite law which associates with every natural number n a corresponding approximate value of the series, the nth partial sum. But law is a static concept. If we ask what is meant by the convergence of the sequence of points $P_1, P_2, \ldots P_n, \ldots$ toward the point P, analysis supplies the answer: it means that for every positive fraction ε there exists a natural number N such that the distance PP_n is smaller than ε for all indices $n \geq N$. The dynamics of the transition to the limit is here reflected in a static relation between the sequence $\{P_n\}$ and the point P, a relation which indeed can only be formulated by an unrestricted use of the terms "there exists" and "all" in connection with the sequence of natural numbers. This standpoint characterizes what was previously called the fourth stage of arithmetic. Consider the definition "n is an even or an odd number according as there exists or does not exist a number x for which $n=2x$." For one who accepts this definition with its appeal to the infinite totality of numbers x as having a meaning, the sequence of numbers open into infinity has transformed itself into a closed aggregate of objects existing in themselves, a realm of absolute existence which "is not of this world," and of which the eye of our consciousness perceives but reflected gleams. In this absolute realm the *tertium non datur* is valid with regard to every property P predicable of numbers. This implies the alternative: either there exists a number of the property P, or all numbers have the opposite property non-P. But this could be decided in all circumstances only if one could examine the entire sequence of numbers with regard to the property P, which contradicts the nature of the infinite. We are therefore prohibited from interpreting an existential proposition as the completed logical sum:* "1 has the property P, or 2, or 3, or . . . in *infinitum*," and from interpreting the general proposition as the logical product: "1 has the property non-P, and 2, and 3, and . . . in *infinitum*." But then the general proposition can only be understood hypothetically as asserting something only if a definite number is given, and it is therefore not deniable. The existential proposition then has a meaning only with regard to a definite example: this definite number constructed in such and such a way has the property P. Existential absolutism disregards such difficulties which spring from the nature of the infinite, and accepts these propositions as ordinary judgments capable of negation and opposing one another in the *tertium non datur*.

The theory of sets, in its endeavor to establish a foundation for analysis, has to go much further: it applies the terms "there exists" and "all" without

* Following Leibniz, I place here the logical combination by "or" in analogy to the arithmetical $+$, combination by "and" in analogy to $\times$.

limitation also to the possible sequences and sets of natural numbers—implying that such propositions refer to an actual state of affairs which lies decided within the things themselves as by "Yes" or "No," even if mathematical investigation may succeed only through a lucky chance in transforming this latent answer into an articulate one. We speak of the set of all even numbers, the set of all prime numbers. A set is thus always described as follows: the set of all numbers of such and such a property; the set is considered as given if a definite criterion decides which elements belong to it and which do not. But if the question arises whether among all possible sets and sequences a set of such and such a kind exists, one can hardly help feeling that through the determination of the "accessible" sets and sequences by laws, a chaotic abundance of possibilities, of "lawless" sets, "arbitrarily thrown together" is lost, and that thereby the clear alternative "does there or does there not exist?" is confused. The theory of sets unhesitatingly makes use of such alternatives in the criteria which it sets up to decide whether a point or a number belongs to a set or not. One can see that it thereby becomes involved in fatal logical circles. It is true that so far no actual contradictions in analysis proper have resulted; we do not completely understand this fact at present. G. Cantor, however, cast off all bonds by operating absolutely freely with the notion of sets, and in particular by permitting that from every set the set of all its subsets may be formed. And only here at the very outskirts of the theory of sets does one incur actual contradictions. Their root, however, must be traced to the bold act mathematics has performed from its very start: treating a field of constructive possibilities like a closed ensemble of objects existing in themselves.

The criticism of H. Poincaré, B. Russell, and mainly Brouwer during the last thirty years has gradually opened our eyes to the untenable logical position from which the method of the theory of sets started out. To my mind, there can no longer be any doubt that this third attempt has also failed—failed in the sense in which it was undertaken. I shall therefore consider now the fourth and last attempt. As D. Hilbert recognized, mathematics may be saved without diminishing its classical content only by a radically new interpretation through a formalization which, in principle, transforms it from a system of knowledge into a game with signs and formulas played according to fixed rules. By extending the symbolic representation customary in mathematics to the logical operations "and," "or," "there exists," and so forth, every mathematical proposition is transformed into a meaningless formula composed of signs, and mathematics itself into a game of formulas regulated by certain conventions—comparable indeed to the game of chess. To the men in the chess game corresponds a limited—or unlimited—supply of signs in mathematics; to an arbitrary position of the men on the board, the combination of the signs into a formula. One formula or several formulas are considered as axioms; their counterpart in the game

of chess is the prescribed position of the men at the
beginning of the game. And as in chess a new position is produced from the preceding one by a move
that has to satisfy certain rules, so in the case of
mathematics, formal rules of conclusion are set down
according to which new formulas can be obtained,
i.e., "deduced" from given ones. Certain formulas of
intuitively described characteristics are branded as
contradictions; in the chess game we may consider
as a "contradiction" any position in which, for example, more than eight white pawns occur. So far
all is game and not cognition. But in "metamathematics," as Hilbert says, the game itself becomes the
object of cognition: we want to know that a contradiction can never occur as the terminal formula of a
proof. This consistency of classical analysis and not
its truth is what Hilbert wishes to insure; the truth
we have renounced, of course, by abandoning its interpretation as a system of significant propositions.
Analogously it is no longer game but cognition,
when one proves that in a correctly played chess
game more than eight white pawns are impossible.
This is done in the following way. At the beginning
there are eight pawns; by a move corresponding to
the rules, the number of pawns can never be increased; ergo . . . This ergo stands for a conclusion by complete induction which follows the moves
of the given game step by step to the final position.
Hilbert needs significative thinking only to obtain
this one cognition; his consistency proof, in principle, is conducted like the one just carried through

for the chess game, although of course it is much
more complicated. It is clear that in these considerations the limitations set by Brouwer for significative
thinking are respected.

From this formalistic standpoint the question as
to a deeper reason for the adopted axioms and rules
of operation is as meaningless as it is in the chess
game. It even remains obscure why it is of concern to
us that the game shall be consistent. All objections
are obviated, since nothing is asserted; rejection
could only take the form of the declaration: I will
not join in the game. If mathematics would seriously
retire to this status of pure game for the sake of its
safety, it would no longer be a determining factor
in the history of the mind. De facto it has not performed this abdication and will not perform it.
Hence we must after all attempt to reassign to
mathematics some function in the service of knowledge. Hilbert expresses himself somewhat obscurely
to the effect that the infinite plays the part of an
idea in the Kantian sense, supplementing the concrete in the sense of totality. If my understanding is
correct, this function is analogous to the act by
which I supplement the objects actually given to me
in my consciousness to form the totality of an objective world, which also comprises many things that
are not immediately before me.

The scientific formulation of this objective conception of the world takes place in physics, which
employs mathematics as a means of construction. But
the situation that prevails in theoretical physics in

no way corresponds to Brouwer's ideal of a science, to his postulate that every proposition shall have its individual meaning, and that this meaning shall be capable of intuitive display. On the contrary, the propositions and laws of physics taken individually do not have a content which can be verified experimentally; it is only the theoretical system as a whole which can be confronted with experience. What is achieved is not intuitive cognition of an individual or general state of facts, and a description which faithfully portrays the given conditions, but theoretical, purely symbolical construction of the world.

The considerations of all three lectures lead from different directions to this basic view. Taking the most primitive object of mathematics, the sequence of natural numbers, as an example, I have outlined the transition from description which merely subsumes the actually occurring numbers under descriptive characteristics and relations to the construction of a field of possibilities which is open into infinity. The latter is precisely the quantitative method of physics; it does not, for example, classify the given colors as Linnaeus classified the actually occurring plants; but it reduces them to the scale of wavelengths, that is, it embeds them in a continuum constructed according to the above described division scheme, in which every possible color must find its place. We found in the second lecture that elementary analysis must be carried so far as to establish elements varying each exclusively within a range of possibilities which can be surveyed from the start, because it originates from free construction. This is one side of the matter which I designated by the term constructive generation of a field of variation. The other side which here mainly interests us is the fact that the subsumption of the particular concrete case, the "individual," into this field does not take place on the basis of immediately recognizable characteristics, but as the result of mental or physical manipulations or reactions to be performed on it. To determine number, for example, one has to apply the process of counting; to determine the mass of a body one has to allow it to react with other bodies and apply the law of momentum to the impact. But this analytical method furnishes "ideal attributes" and not concrete properties. We ascribe these ideal attributes to the objects, even if the manipulations necessary to "measure" them are not really carried out. If we indicate the distance of the sun from the earth in feet, this statement would acquire a meaning verifiable in the given state of facts only if a rigid pole on which the individual division had been marked by laying off a movable, rigid measuring rod were so applied on the earth that its end touched the sun. But this rigid pole between earth and sun does not exist, the measurement by a rigid rod is not really carried out. Geometrical statements of this kind consequently lack a meaning that can be exhibited in the given facts; the network of ideal determinations touches experiential reality only here and there, but at these points of contact ideal determination and experience must agree. Quantum theory has shown that the transformation of the results of possible reactions into properties is precarious. One may without hesitation combine two properties with each other by "and," but not so the results of two measurements, if the performance of one makes the performance of the other impossible in principle.

To illustrate what the required concordance between theory and experience consists of, let us take the following example, chosen as simple as possible. We observe one single oscillation of a pendulum; let us assume that it is possible to observe its duration directly with an error of .1 second, so that periods of oscillation differing theoretically by less than .1 second are actually equal for our direct perception. There is, however, a simple means of increasing the exactness one hundred fold: one waits until 100 oscillations have taken place and divides the observed time interval by 100. But this indirect determination is dependent on an assumption, namely that all individual oscillations take the same time. This can of course be tested with an exactness of .1 second by direct observation. But that is not meant here. We wish instead to assert that the periods of oscillation are absolutely equal or equal with hundred fold precision. This assumption, as well as the assertion concerning the duration of an individual oscillation, is meaningless for the intuitionist who respects the limits of intuitive exactness. Still, a test of the theory is possible in a certain sense: one finds that the duration of m successive oscillations is to that of n oscillations as $m:n$, when m and n are large numbers. (For the test several series of consecutive oscillations are

arbitrarily chosen.) In general the matter is as follows: through the exact laws of the theory which is
taken as a basis, the quantity x to be determined is
placed in functional dependence on a number of
other quantities. By observing these quantities conclusions can be drawn as to the value of x, which per-
mit us to ascertain x more precisely than is possible
by its direct observation. The underlying theory is
considered to hold good, if within the limits of error
to be expected all indirect methods of determining x
lead to the same result. But every such indirect determination, every distinction not existing for intuitive perception, is possible only on the ground of
theories. These theories can only be verified by observing that when tested in all their numerical consequences, they furnish concordance within the limits
of error.

It is a deep philosophical question, what "truth"
or objectivity we are to assign to theoretical construction as it extends far beyond the actually
given. The concordance just discussed is an indis-
pensable requirement that every theory must satisfy.
It includes, however, the consistency of the theory,
so that here also we receive a rational answer to the
question as to why the consistency of formalized
mathematics is of importance to us: it is that part
of concordance which relates only to the theory itself,
the part in which the theory is not yet confronted
with experience. It is the task of the mathematician
to see that the theories of the concrete sciences satisfy this condition *sine qua non:* that they be for-
mally definite and consistent. My opinion may be

summed up as follows: if mathematics is taken by
itself, one should restrict oneself with Brouwer to the
intuitively cognizable truths and consider the infinite
only as an open field of possibilities; nothing com-
pels us to go farther. But in the natural sciences we
are in contact with a sphere which is impervious to
intuitive evidence; here cognition necessarily becomes
symbolical construction. Hence we need no longer demand that when mathematics is taken into the process of theoretical construction in physics it should
be possible to set apart the mathematical element as
a special domain in which all judgments are intuitively certain; from this higher viewpoint which
makes the whole of science appear as one unit, I consider Hilbert to be right.

In concluding I shall try to put together in a few
general theses the experiences which mathematics has
gained in the course of its history by an investigation
of the infinite.

(1) In the spiritual life of man two domains are
clearly to be distinguished from one another: on one
side the domain of creation (*Gestaltung*), of construction, to which the active artist, the scientist, the
technician, the statesman devote themselves; on the
other side the domain of reflection (*Besinnung*)
which consummates itself in cognitions and which one
may consider as the specific realm of the philosopher.
The danger of constructive activity unguided by reflection is that it departs from meaning, goes astray,
stagnates in mere routine; the danger of passive reflection is that it may lead to incomprehensible "talk-

ing about things" which paralyzes the creative power of man. What we were engaged in here was reflection. Hilbert's mathematics as well as physics belongs in the domain of constructive action; metamathematics, however, with its cognition of consistency, belongs to reflection.

(2) The task of science can surely not be performed through intuitive cognition alone, since the objective sphere with which it deals is by its very nature impervious to reason. But even in pure mathematics, or in pure logic, we cannot decide the validity of a formula by means of descriptive characteristics. We must resort to action: we start out from the axioms and apply the practical rules of conclusion in arbitrarily frequent repetition and combination. In this sense one can speak of an original darkness of reason: we do not have truth, we do not perceive it if we merely open our eyes wide, but truth must be attained by action.

(3) The infinite is accessible to the mind intuitively in the form of the field of possibilities open into infinity, analogous to the sequence of numbers which can be continued indefinitely; but

(4) the completed, the actual infinite as a closed realm of absolute existence is not within its reach.

(5) Yet the demand for totality and the metaphysical belief in reality inevitably compel the mind to represent the infinite as closed being by symbolical construction.

I take these experiences derived from the develop-

ment of mathematics seriously in a philosophical
sense. The mathematical tendencies which first an-
nounced themselves with Nicolaus of Cusa have, as I
have tried to explain, been elaborated in the course
of the centuries and have reached their fulfilment. I
therefore ask you to consider the content of this lecture as a more precise exposition referring back to
what I said in the first lecture concerning the mathematical and theological ideas of Nicolaus of Cusa. If,
following his steps, we may undertake to give a theological formulation to our last three conclusions, we
may say this:

We reject the thesis of the categorical finiteness
of man, both in the atheistic form of obdurate finiteness which is so alluringly represented today in Ger-
many by the Freiburg philosopher Heidegger, and
in the theistic, specifically Lutheran-Protestant form,
where it serves as a background for the violent
drama of contrition, revelation and grace. On the
contrary, mind is freedom within the limitations of
existence; it is open toward the infinite. Indeed, God
as the completed infinite cannot and will not be com-
prehended by it; neither can God penetrate into man
by revelation, nor man penetrate to him by mystical
perception. The completed infinite we can only represent in symbols. From this relationship every creative act of man receives its deep consecration and
dignity. But only in mathematics and physics, as far
as I can see, has symbolical-theoretical construction
acquired sufficient solidity to be convincing for
everyone whose mind is open to these sciences.